REFLECTIONS

REFLECTIONS

J. DOUGLAS BARRY

Reflections

Copyright © 2019 by J. Douglas Barry. All rights reserved.

No part of this publication may be reproduced, stored in a retrieval system or transmitted in any way by any means, electronic, mechanical, photocopy, recording or otherwise without the prior permission of the author except as provided by USA copyright law.

The opinions expressed by the author are not necessarily those of URLink Print and Media.

1603 Capitol Ave., Suite 310 Cheyenne, Wyoming USA 82001
1-888-980-6523 | admin@urlinkpublishing.com

URLink Print and Media is committed to excellence in the publishing industry.

Book design copyright © 2019 by URLink Print and Media. All rights reserved.

Published in the United States of America
ISBN 978-1-64367-375-2 (Paperback)
ISBN 978-1-64367-376-9 (Hardback)
ISBN 978-1-64367-374-5 (Digital)
29.04.19

To Saman and Sarin and saint Jacinta Marto of Fatima

Contents

1. The Desert Within 9
2. The Visitation 15
3. Celibacy 19
4. Obedience and Respect 23
5. Martha and Mary 25
6. The Love of God 29
7. Agony in the Garden 33
8. His Most Precious Blood 37
9. On Life 41
10. The Last Miracle 45
11. On the Different Levels of Experiencing God 49
12. The Descent of the Holy Spirit 53
13. My Personal Search for the Face of God 55
14. Meditations on the Holy Rosary 61

1
THE DESERT WITHIN

CHRIST CALLS EACH of us to embrace him by deepening our personal experience of him through both prayer and liturgy. An awareness of God in the Trinity allows us to enter into the desert where Christ truly lives. He does not live there alone but rather in every person we see.

Some, such as those living in a monastic environment, have chosen to search for God in the solitary life. The community in which they live promotes a truly "desert" environment. Others, those who are members of a religious organization but who live outside a monastic enclosure, experience the "desert" through the occasional retreat that they make to either a monastery or a retreat house.

There is a third group, one in minority that is neither in the monastic setting nor a member of a religious community, working among the poor, elderly, or just those in need. This latter group is made up of individuals with little or no group support who have chosen to give their life to God by helping anyone in need. Through their charity, they have come to know Christ, for it is he who has called them.

Eventually, this charity or love of others will bring them to know God on a deeper level, even if they initially began to help others just for the sake of helping them and not necessarily as a conscious effort to follow Christ. For it is Christ who has planted the seed of love in their hearts, and this love will at some point bring a conscious realization that it is in Christ and for Christ that their every act of charity has its origin.

Once a conscious awareness of Christ dwelling within them has taken place, a searching, even a longing, for greater knowledge of him takes root within their being. This is not an overnight process but rather one that takes many years of nurturing.

Liturgy, spiritual reading, and personal prayer play an important part of experiencing Christ. We must remember that it is in Scripture that we read "So faith, hope love abide, these three; but the greatest of these is love" (1 Corinthians 13:13). We read further, "…so faith, apart from works is dead" (James 2:26). Most importantly, when Christ was asked what the two greatest commandments were, his response was "you shall love the Lord your God with all your heart, and with all your soul, and with all your mind….And a second is like it, you shall love your neighbor as yourself " (Matt. 23:37–40). For they who are out in the world helping others with all their heart are also truly loving God with their whole being by their very actions.

He who sees their love now calls them to knowledge and to a personal awareness of he who is love. It is at this moment that the individual so called enters into the desert to experience Christ. As this deepening awareness takes place, one begins to notice certain changes. At liturgy, for example, when one says, "Lord, I am not worthy to receive you. Speak but the word, and my soul shall be healed,"* he realizes that although he perceives other voices speaking, all he really hears is his own voice speaking directly to God. The reception of the Eucharist then becomes a very personal experience. The taking of body and blood unites the communicant into a further awareness of Christ now dwelling within.

---

* This is from the Catholic Liturgy that finds its origin in Matt. 8:8.

Reflections

When the liturgy is over and one physically leaves the place of worship, it is not necessary to leave the desert behind. It is, rather, so much more important to remain in the desert at all times. For it is here that we find Christ, and with Christ, we can accomplish so much more in our dealings with others.

"Greater love has no man than this, that a man lay down his life for his friends" (John 15:13). Christ freely laid down his life for us as an example to us of how we should live.

Through sin, we lose some of our love. But not all, for it is the love of God that causes us to seek repentance. Sin is common to all. Sin is fun. Sin is pleasurable. Sin offers us so much more excitement than "non-sin." Sin deceives, for sin hurts and rejects the love that comes from God. In many instances, sin also hurts our neighbor. Sin is in fact a lie! The seeking of forgiveness brings us back to him, who had already forgiven our sins before we ask, so great is his love for us. With each fall and subsequent return to Christ, with humble hearts, we strengthen our resolve to continue in our quest of oneness with him and to avoid sin at all costs.

We now return to the desert, firm in our resolve to stay longer, for sin and desert cannot coexist. In Christ, there is no sin, and Christ is in the desert. If we want to stay with him in the desert, then we must resist all sin. The longer we experience him in the desert, the longer we will want to stay. "Until now you have asked nothing in my name; ask, and you will receive, that your joy may be full" (John 16:24). This joy is given to us through the Holy Spirit, the third person of the Trinity. If you ask, the Holy Spirit will bring you closer to God the Father.

> "If a man loves me, he will keep my word, and my father will love him, and we will come to him and make our home with him." (John 14:23)

It is this indwelling that gives us joy. It is Christ within that brings us to a true realization, through the Holy Spirit, of who God really is. We must seek him in the desert and subsequently carry the Holy Trinity out of the desert to others. As we carry the Holy Trinity out of the desert, we must remain personally within the desert so that others might experience the presence of God within through our love and works of charity.

God has knowledge of our heart's desire, and Scripture states that to his faithful, he will give their heart's desire. Many say, How can this be? For there are those whose heart's desire goes against the teaching of Christ. Yet this is not a problem! If the Holy Spirit through Scripture has promised our heart's desire to the faithful, then rest assured it shall be. One need only to strive toward overcoming sin and following Christ. God loves us so much that even in this life we can experience moments of our heart's desire, which brings great contentment and inner peace.

This does not mean that if my heart's desire is to sin, I can go out and freely sin without any concern for love of God or neighbor. God forbid! Sin brings great remorse, if not at first then at some point in our life. We can either react to the remorse we feel and repent or reject it and fall even deeper into sin. The decision to reject the remorse we feel and continue in sin causes the indwelling of the Holy Spirit to cease. Should we never return to God or hold stubbornly on to our sins, then we do so to our own destruction.

People talk of the pains and terrors of hell. Yet the greatest pain, the greatest terror, is not a physical one but rather the knowledge of the great love that God has for us having been lost for all eternity. For it is this love that God overshadows us with at the moment of our judgment, and by then it is too late. Truly, there would be great wailing and weeping and gnashing of teeth.

Reflections

Now is the time to experience God's love. Now is the time to embrace him so that he and his Son, our Lord Jesus Christ, can make their dwelling within us. But it is an invitation that we must make, an invitation that is in response to the Holy Spirit knocking, an invitation to come in and love.

—November 12, 1993

2

THE VISITATION

A YOUNG WOMAN SITS alone—a girl, really, of about fourteen to sixteen years of age. An angel from God appears to her, which is in itself an extraordinary event. The angel, Gabriel, tells of an even greater event about to take place: that she, Mary, a virgin, "will conceive in your womb and bear a Son, and you shall call his name Jesus" (Luke 1:31).

Mary, of course, was amazed. How could such a thing be? She was betrothed but not yet married, and she was in fact a virgin. "How will this be, since I do not know man?" (Luke 1:34) "The Holy Spirit will come upon you, and the power of the Most High will overshadow you; therefore the child to be born will be called holy, the Son of God" (Luke 1:35).

The angel must have known how overwhelmed Mary would be with such an announcement for he went on to state, "And behold, your kinswoman Elizabeth in her old age has also conceived a son; and this is the sixth month with her who was called barren. For with God nothing will be impossible" (Luke 1:36–37). And Mary said, "Behold, I am the handmaid of the Lord; let it be to me according to your word" (Luke 1:38). There is no doubt in that sentence, just total acceptance. Yet a rational person would wonder at the amazement of it all. There had to be confirmation! God in his infinite wisdom would have realized this, and therefore, another event of almost equal proportions had to occur. We have, therefore, the conception of a child to a woman too old to conceive. Mary goes in haste to the town of Judah—perhaps to give support to her kinswoman in her time of need, as may have been the custom at that time, but also perhaps to put to rest any lingering doubt as to her own condition.

If Mary truly had any doubts, they were immediately put to rest with the greeting of Elizabeth: "Blest are you among women and blest is the fruit of your womb" (Luke 1:42). There is no mention in Holy Scripture that Mary inquired if Elizabeth was pregnant or stated that she believed herself to be. The Scripture tells us that Elizabeth's words were in response to "Mary's greeting." How could Elizabeth know that Mary had conceived? Then, to give further support, Elizabeth continues: "And why is this granted me, that the mother of my Lord should come to me?" (Luke 1:43) The mystery, the glorious mystery, comes to the front: "The Mother of my Lord." Truly, here stands the mother of the one true God, who has been and is yet to be, through the birth that Mary is about to give. "For behold, when the voice of your greeting came to my ears, the child in my womb leapt for joy" (Luke 1:44). Finally, all doubt ceases, for now Mary has it confirmed that this old woman has conceived. The angel was real, not a hallucination. The impossible has occurred: not only has an old woman conceived but a virgin as well.

Elizabeth, being the elder, then speaks for both: "And blessed is she who believed that there would be a fulfilment of what was spoken to her from the Lord." (Luke 1:45).

Mary then goes on to acknowledge and totally accept her condition, her love of God, his greatness, his might, his wonder, his goodness, and her humility as she proclaims instantaneously her canticle in Luke 1:46–55:

The Magnificat

"My soul magnifies the Lord,
and my spirit rejoices in God my Savior;
for he has regarded the low estate of his handmaiden.
For behold, henceforth all generations will call me blessed,
for he who is mighty has done great things
for me, and holy is his name.
And his mercy is on those who fear him
from generation to generation.
He has shown strength with his arm,
he has scattered the proud in the imagination of their hearts,
he has put down the mighty from their
thrones, and exalted those of low degree;
he has filled the hungry with good things,
and the rich he has sent empty away."
(Luke 1:46-53)

—February 11, 1995

3
CELIBACY

CELIBACY MAY BE the single most difficult state that anyone could ever attempt to achieve. For a single individual in a religious setting, to have taken a vow of celibacy is one thing. They have the support of their community. But for an individual who has not taken a vow of celibacy and who does not belong to a religious community, the difficulty appears to be even greater.

To be celibate—totally celibate, which means no sexual pleasure at all—is to do so for Christ. Yet being celibate for Christ does not make the act any easier. There are so many different sexual pleasures existing that the struggle of celibacy is extremely difficult. Even without the aid of a partner, there is self-gratification that brings on an orgasm.

There are sexual thoughts that can lead to self-stimulation, which in turn will lead to orgasm. There are pleasures of the eye that trigger thought that leads to masturbation that leads to orgasm.

All of these—pictures, thought, self-stimulation—will lead the individual to seek out sexual fulfillment with a partner. Yet, we should remember: "For the wages of sin is death, but the free gift of God is eternal life in Christ Jesus our Lord" (Romans 6:23).

For one to achieve total celibacy certain goals must be sought—the most obvious of these being not wanting to lose one's soul. Self-preservation is our greatest instinct, and although we do not expect to die within the immediate future, we know that someday we will. Therefore we make somewhat of a struggle to be pleasing to God.

This is not, however, enough for us to achieve total celibacy. We need more. We must rise above self- preservation and be celibate for no other reason than for Christ. We take our sacrifice and unite it to God's only Son on the cross.

> "For God so loved the world that he gave his only-begotten son, that whoever believes in him should not perish but have eternal life." (John 3:16)

How deep is a parent's love for their child! For a parent to lose a child is the greatest of all losses. The total devastation that one experiences when a child dies is more than any parent can bear. The faith that tells us that we will be reunited with our child is of little comfort when that child we loved so much has left us to endure our agony alone.

And so it is with God. He—the Supreme Being, yes—who knew that his Son would be with him shortly in glory suffered at the death of his only Son.

Was not the earth covered in darkness, and did not the earth quake at the hour of Christ's death? Was not the veil of the temple torn in two when Christ died on the cross? Truly, the Supreme Being, whose love is beyond all understanding, was in sorrow the moment his Son died.

What is most incredible, however, is that despite the knowledge God had that his Son would undergo such an ignominious death, his love for us and his desire for our salvation was so great that he permitted his Son to die on the cross so that we might achieve salvation.

Reflections

Taking all this into account, for those who choose not to marry but to remain single for Christ, can not celibacy also be our gift to such a loving Father as our Supreme Being?

Should we fail at our attempt, we must then begin again in sorrow. As David writes in Psalm 51: "...my sin is ever before me." (51:3) "...blot out all my iniquities." (51:9) "...a broken and contrite heart, O God, you will not despise." (51:17)

Each time we begin anew, we become a little stronger in our resolve not to sin. Should we fall a hundred times, we will be a hundred times stronger to resist the temptation to sin. With faith, we proceed, pleasing to God, in our attempt to be pleasing to him.

When your own child disappoints you, or perhaps not a child but someone you deeply care for has done something to offend you, do you not forgive them and continue in your love for them? How much more will our Father in heaven, whose knowledge is beyond all comprehension, love us when we strive, though weak and sinful, to please him?

Though sin offends God, our repentance pleases him. Better if we never sinned at all. But when we do, the remorse we feel comes from God's love for us. If God did not love us, we would never feel remorse. It is up to us then to respond to remorse and bring our contrite heart to the doorstep of God's loving heart. As we begin again now in the state of God's grace, we become stronger in our battle to be celibate. With the struggle to please God comes gentle wisdom—for example, suggestive thoughts to rise early in the morning for prayer and to avoid certain situations that we know beforehand will lead us into sin.

The tools to achieve our goal are also present. We have the Holy Scripture, the Liturgy of the Hours, daily Mass, and the Holy Eucharist. In addition to this, we also have the Holy Rosary and frequent reconciliation. We must avail ourselves of these gifts of God, who understands our struggle. If we attempt to struggle alone, without the holy gifts that God has made available to us, then we will never succeed. But if we avail ourselves of his gifts, not only will we succeed in our struggle to please him, but we will also grow closer to God. We will do what Christ has exhorted us to do in the Gospel of John: "If a man loves me, he will keep my word, and my Father will love him, and we will come to him and make our home with him" (John 14:23).

—February 17, 1994

4
OBEDIENCE AND RESPECT

Holy Scripture has much to tell us through the written word. There is, however, much that is unwritten yet still discernable through prayer, thought, and, finally, revelation. There are stories such as the finding in the temple and the wedding feast in Cana that are connected through the unwritten word.

Let us remember that Christ is the Word made flesh, so he is also the unwritten word yet more difficult to find.

In the finding in the temple, we have a twelve-year-old boy turning to his parents, Mary and Joseph, and almost chastising them with his statement: "…How is it that you sought me? Did you not know that I must be in my Father's house?" (John 2:49)

What is not written here is the response that Mary and Joseph would have given to a twelve-year-old child speaking in such a way. It is possible that Mary would have responded in the following manner: "I know that you are a very special person and that your birth was special. But a twelve-year-old boy does not need to be speaking to his parents in such a way. We are responsible for your well- being and safety, and your father and I were upset that we could not find you. I know that Joseph is not your real father. But for now, he is your father on earth, and you must be obedient to him and me. The time for your ministry is not now. You are only a boy. When the time is right, your Father in heaven will let you know."

The very next passage is that Jesus went down into Nazareth and was obedient to them. It goes on to state that he grew in wisdom and grace. The stage had been set. Mary and Joseph had to teach Jesus obedience and respect if he were to truly succeed.

In John 2, we see the first miracle of Jesus: the changing of the water into wine at Cana. Here again, Mary plays an important role as a mother.

Mary approaches Jesus to tell him that the guests were out of wine. She truly knew who he was. Jesus's response was one of protest. "O woman, what have you to do with me? My hour has not yet come" (John 2:4). Mary turns to the waiters and says, "Do whatever he tells you" (John 2:5).

Mary knew that Jesus was the obedient son. She knew that not only would Jesus do as she requested but also that he had the capability to perform the miracle needed. By her request to Jesus, she was perhaps telling him that his time had indeed come. He in return responded to the loving mother who had taught him both obedience and respect.

If Mary had not taught Jesus to respect and be obedient to his parents in the "finding in the temple," then perhaps this miracle—that is, the changing of water into wine—would never have taken place. Jesus's ministry might have taken a different direction.

The finding in the temple and the wedding feast in Cana are therefore related through the loving hand of Jesus's mother, Mary. The teaching of obedience and respect in the temple manifested itself at the wedding feast in Cana.

—January 12, 1994

5
MARTHA AND MARY

"MARTHA, MARTHA, YOU are anxious and troubled about many things; one thing is needful. Mary has chosen the good portion, which shall not be taken away from her" (Luke 10:41–42). Thus was Jesus's response to Martha's complaint that her sister Mary had been sitting doing nothing except listening to the words of Jesus while she went about with great effort preparing the tasks of hospitality.

Two opposing issues are taken from this scripture. One side uses the scriptural passage to promote the idea of and call to contemplation—that is, Mary's choice to sit at the Lord's feet and listen to his words. The other side states that if it were not for the efforts of Martha, Mary would not have been able to contemplate Jesus's words. The latter position then promotes the active life. Both active and contemplative are necessary and pleasing to our Lord. We have, however, a very interesting and profound statement by Jesus:

"Mary has chosen the good portion." (Luke 10:42)

Perhaps there is, therefore, a third aspect that has not been looked at as closely as the first two: that it is necessary for both Mary and Martha to listen to his teaching. In a broader perspective, it would be better for all religious and nonreligious to contemplate the words of our Lord.

Jesus knew that there would come a time for them to eat, to break bread together. He stated:

> "Therefore do not be anxious, saying, 'what shall we eat?' or 'what shall we drink?' or 'what shall we wear?' For the gentiles seek all these things; and your heavenly Father knows that you need them all. But seek first his kingdom and his righteousness, and all these things shall be yours as well." (Matt. 6:31–34)

"Seek his way of holiness." This is what Mary had been doing and what Martha should have been doing. Then instead of being told that her much ado was not as important, she could have been refreshed at the Lord's feet in contemplation. When Jesus had finished speaking, the three of them could have risen together and prepared the meal or whatever else may have been necessary.

Community and contemplation are both important, but not, if we take Jesus at his word—equally so. Seeking after holiness through contemplation is of greatest importance. Having completed a period of contemplation, we then return to community.

Jesus knew, through his own experience as a man, that it would be necessary to strengthen the day, each day, by first seeking holiness and dwelling upon his words.

Before he began his preaching in Galilee, he spent forty days in the desert. The devil then tempted Jesus. "If you are the Son of God, command this stone to become bread" (Luke 4:3). Jesus, of course, rejected Satan's temptation: "It is written, 'Man shall not live by bread alone'" (Luke 4:4).

Reflections

There were other temptations that Jesus quickly overcame. In his temptation of Jesus, Satan, knowing who Jesus was, went after the human condition of the Son of God. His divinity could not be touched, but his humanity could. We have, therefore, the tempting of not only the senses through hunger but of pride and avarice as well. Jesus, through his fasting and prayer of forty days, had prepared his human state to resist the temptations of Satan. In his statement to Martha that "Mary has chosen the good portion," (Luke 10:42) he exhorts all of mankind to prepare through listening to his words, seeking holiness, and contemplation for the trials and tribulations of each day.

As we grow in holiness and thus wisdom as did Jesus at the conclusion of his successful encounter with the devil: "And Jesus returned in the power of the Spirit into Galilee…" (Luke 4:14), we shall be able to overcome our own temptations in life. Whether we begin each day in contemplation, at Mass and Holy Eucharist, or by saying the Rosary, we will better be able to prepare the tasks of hospitality.

Scripture does not say what Martha, Mary, and Jesus did after Jesus had spoken to Martha, but his words were eternal to all those who would hear them down through the ages:

> "…Mary has chosen the good portion, which shall not be taken away from her." (Luke 10:42)

—February 12, 1995

6
THE LOVE OF GOD

"...You shall love the Lord your God with all your heart, and with all your soul, and with all your mind, and with all your strength. The second is this, 'you shall love your neighbor as yourself'" (Mark 12:30–31) is a means by which we can also love God above all else.

We want happiness and freedom from want. We may not achieve this in our lives, but in our next lives, we can. When Christ came on earth, he used parables to tell of the joys of heaven and what we must do to achieve heaven. In the Old Testament, particularly in Psalms, we are told that God will give to his faithful their hearts' desires.

People naturally focus on the self, the all-important "I." The Holy Spirit, being aware of this, teaches through Scripture for man to be good and faithful. Through loyalty to Christ, we will be rewarded.

The true importance of God, the Supreme Being who has never been seen or whose true qualities have never been realized, is not appreciated by man. We might rationalize that to lose a loved one would be devastating, especially a child. Yet we never seem to rationalize that to lose God would be the most devastating experience we could ever undergo.

The people in our lives are tangible. We see, touch, and love actual beings with real body and real blood. The love we give is returned to us in a concrete way, and we come to know and appreciate that love received. Yet the love of God should be paramount in our life. The love he gives in return is the greatest of all loves, yet we don't truly appreciate that love (except for a few extraordinary saints who do) unless we experience him in his kingdom, the kingdom of heaven.

This problem of ours—to only love that which we know as real through our actual experiences—is manifested throughout Scripture.

The Holy Spirit promises us that if we perform certain actions, we shall achieve salvation. By doing so, the Holy Spirit is showing an awareness of man's weakness. It is not enough to say "Love God!" Promises of rewards for loving God must be given.

The dilemma is this: our self-centeredness requires us to seek a goal but only if we know beforehand that we will greatly be rewarded. Christ tells of "jewels in a crown," "mansions in heaven," and "our heart's desire." What we should really be doing is loving God and his Son Jesus Christ for no other reason than to love him. We should not, in our love of God, look for a reward; for by so doing, we run the danger of having the desire of that reward obscure our love of God. In fact, the love of self can get in the way when we consider our heart's desire.

We manifest our love of God through the carrying out of his second commandment: "Love thy neighbor as thy self." But do we perform this action because we know we will receive a great reward if we do? Or do we do it just for the love of God and neighbor without any consideration of reward? It is the latter response that we should have.

To focus on God and him alone should be our sole intent. To carry out his desires by keeping his commandments and loving his Son should be paramount for the sake of God and for no other reason. We must love God only for the sake of loving God. We should not consider self in the love of God but rather put our whole trust in him. To ask "What's in it for me?" is a very human response, and God understands this. To put our humanness aside and to focus on God alone would be a greater accomplishment and a greater love that would be more pleasing to God.

—January 28, 1994

7
AGONY IN THE GARDEN

THE GOD YOU seek is the God you will more than likely find. The Cistercian monks, for example, seek a God who is loving, yes, but one who demands solitude, silence, austerity, loneliness, self-discipline, penance, fasting, and other hardships that will lead hopefully and eventually to a profoundly deep spirituality.

But God is not only that kind of a god. Though he is but one God and three persons in one God, the primary person—that is, the Father—can also be an extremely compassionate and loving god, a god who does not demand solitude and loneliness but also joy and companionship. There is Christ in the desert and Christ in the Agony in the Garden, but there is also Christ who had Lazarus, Mary, and Martha as his friends. There is the Christ who had companions, his disciples, with whom he ate, drank, and spoke at great length. Finally, there is the Christ who loved to have the children around him: "Let the children come to me, and do not hinder them, for to such belongs the kingdom of heaven" (Matt. 19–14).

Christ spoke of the Holy Spirit, the third person of the Trinity. He is there for the asking. He, the Holy Spirit, will come to comfort and teach if we but simply ask.

All of this—love and loneliness, companionship and solitude, austerity, self-discipline, penance, and the love for life that all children have—confronted Christ in the Agony in the Garden.

He was God made man! He was given by his Father in heaven to be sacrificed for our sins so that through him, we might have life eternal. But this Son of God was also man. He was a man with friends, friends whom he loved personally. Can any man, woman, or child come into this life and not develop a deep love for another individual? When that relationship comes to an end, by whatever means, do we not feel great sorrow? Could Christ—just because he was Christ, the Savior of the world—have felt any less toward his friends? Did he not cry when he was told that Lazarus had died? They remarked, "…See how he loved him!" (John 11:36) Yet Christ knew he would raise Lazarus from the dead and have this man whom he loved back as a friend once again.

Imagine, therefore, how truly great his agony in the garden must have been. The pain he was to undergo he was truly cognizant of, but this was not his greatest sorrow in the Garden of Gethsemane. His greatest sorrow was the knowledge that he was about to lose the companionship of his friends.

Christ knew that a family (a wife and children) were out of the question. But the love he had for his friends was paramount, for on earth, as man, this was all he had. He knew that he would one day see them again in his Father's kingdom. Yet he knew in his heart that he would see Lazarus again in this life, and still he wept. How much greater, then, was his sorrow the night he was betrayed!

In addition to his sorrow that his comradeship was about to end, there was the agony he felt over his sense of failure. His mission was to "save the world." But this accomplishment did not come about during his lifetime. This mission was no longer up to him. He was to die! It was rather up to his apostles to teach the Way of Christ and for each individual to then choose or not choose whether they would accept this teaching or not.

Reflections

Christ then had one final concern, and that was to rise from the dead; only then would people accept his teachings in faith. He knew he would rise, for in addition to his humanity, we also have his divinity. Christ knew who he was! Yet even in his rising from the dead, there was a doubter, Thomas, who would not believe unless he saw Christ risen.

Christ's experience of sorrow, loss, and failure in the Agony in the Garden helps him to have a better understanding of our own loss, sorrow, and failure in life. His agony was his destiny, yet even that destiny could have been avoided, for Christ, like us, had a free will. It was his choice to suffer for our salvation. He gave up his friends, suffered the pain of death, and underwent great sorrow for our sakes. An easy choice it was not, for he said, "Father, if you are willing, remove this chalice from me" (Luke 22:42). Christ was struggling with the idea that his love for his friends was about to end for what was really total strangers, you and me, but he relented, "nevertheless not my will, but yours, be done" (Luke 22:42).

Perhaps the love that Christ had for his friends also had a bearing on his decision. For he was not only saving our souls by his death but also the souls of his dearly beloved friends.

Christ's agony was necessary as was his death. Perhaps when we are confronted with hardships, we can remember all his sufferings to bring us salvation. We can be consoled by the fact that when we suffer for whatever reason, that suffering is appreciated by Christ for he has already suffered. He knows what we are going through because he has been there himself.

—June 8, 1994

8

His Most Precious Blood

"Unless you eat the flesh of the Son of man and drink his blood, you have no life in you; he who eats my flesh and drinks my blood has eternal life, and I will raise him up at the last day." (John 6:53–56)

AGAIN, IN THE Gospel of Matthew, at the Last Supper, Christ says to his apostles as he gave them the broken bread, "Take, eat; this is my body. And he took a chalice, and when he had given thanks he gave it to them, saying, 'Drink of it, all of you; for this is my blood of the covenant, which is poured out for many for the forgiveness of sins'" (Matt. 26:26–27). It is not "either-or"; it is *both* bread and wine changed into body and blood. His commandment to us is to consume both. When he suffered for us during his Passion, his body was made to suffer, and his blood was spilled. What if Christ had complained, "You can punish my flesh but do not spill my blood." Would our sins have been forgiven? Remember his words: "To be poured out... for the forgiveness of sins" (Matt. 26:27). His blood had to be shed for our salvation.

How many of us today would gladly give all we possess to have been at the foot of the cross with a cup, catching his precious blood as it fell to earth enriching the soil? I dare say all of us! Yet how many people, each week at Mass and in fact every day, receive the body but willingly refuse the blood?

If Christ had refused the second nail in his hand after experiencing the intense pain of the first, something that he had the power to do—remember he was not only man but the Son of God as well—where would our salvation be? But no, he took not only the second nail but the third as well! He suffered asphyxiation on the cross, for this is how one dies in a crucifixion, as well as an immeasurable loss of blood. This he did of his own free choosing for people who would be in fact total strangers—that is, you and me.

So then how can some of us refuse his precious blood of our own free choosing? It's as if we are saying, "No, thank you, Lord. Not today." If we have faith to receive the bread at the Holy Eucharist (which is, in essence, his body), then we should also have faith to receive the wine (in essence his blood, his precious blood, shed for the forgiveness of *our* sins).

Recall his words once again: "He who eats my flesh and drinks my blood has eternal life." (John 6:54). Once again, Christ does not say "either-or"; he says *both*: body and blood.

Perhaps there are excuses here. "I don't like receiving from a cup that someone else has drunk from. I might catch something and get sick." Do you think that Christ enjoyed shedding his blood? How sick must he have been to hang on a cross for three hours? If receiving from a cup from which other people have drunk is distasteful to you, how distasteful do you think Christ's entire Passion, from the Agony in the Garden to the taking of his last breath, must have been to him?

He had a choice. He did not have to suffer. He did not have to die. He said, "For this reason the Father loves me, because I lay down my life, that I may take it again. No one takes it from me, but I lay it down of my own accord" (John 10:17–18). Was it an easy choice? In the Agony in the Garden, Christ said, "Father, if you are willing, remove this chalice from me; nevertheless not my will, but yours, be done" (Luke 22: 42). So it was not an easy choice, yet he chose to do so for his love of us. With knowledge of all this, so many people actually choose to not receive that precious blood that had been shed by Christ.

Others might complain, "I have a bad cold and don't want to spread it." An acceptable reason, but the writer's personal faith and his relationship with the Lord tells him that it is highly unlikely that any sickness and germs of any kind could long survive in the actual blood of Christ. Yes, his very words and our very faith tell us that what we receive is his actual blood each and every time we receive it. For as many people who don't receive his precious blood, there are as many excuses not to receive it, I am sure. Only one answer, however, will be required by Christ of that person who refused to drink his blood. Why? What will be their answer? Can they say, "I didn't know"? Yet at each Mass they attend, the priest says, "Take ye and drink for this is my blood. It will be shed for you and for many so that sins will be forgiven. Do this in memory of me."

It staggers the imagination to think that so many people daily say, "No, thank you, Lord. I would rather not." And they don't!

How many of these same people will be standing at the gate of heaven expecting to be welcomed by the Lord with open arms? Once again, how will they answer his question of "You received my body but not my blood. Why?" Where is their life eternal, their *vitam aeternam*, for not receiving *corporis et Sanguinis Domini nostri Jesu Christi*? It is like telling God that I want only half of your Son, not all of him. When he died on the cross, however, all of him was given. His Sacred Body was punished, and his Most Precious Blood was shed.

Deo gratias!

—July 12, 1995

Postscript

I recently received a host that had a line of red blood through it. The texture was soggy, so I saw and felt a different host. I now know that both body and blood are present in the host. It is, therefore, not necessary to take the cup to receive the blood for it is present in the host. I do feel, however, that when the cup is offered, we should accept it as a courtesy to our Lord. But to each his own. There is certainly no fault in not taking the cup when offered.

I received that special host the morning after a day of great personal suffering.

Deo gratias!

—July 6, 1999

9

ON LIFE

PAIN, SUFFERING, LONELINESS, and sorrow can at times be more than a person can tolerate. In their search for a solution to the problem, many turn to drugs and alcohol for solace. But the answer is not here, so they eventually turn to suicide. In the case of older loved ones who have lost the mental capability to determine their own plight, they resort to what has become known as *euthanasia*. For those who look to God in their time of need, they find little comfort. They reason that a loving and merciful God would be compassionate and forgive their loved one. In so doing, however, they ignore the Scripture that has been written for all time, Scripture that is not just for the time that Christ walked upon the earth but for modern times as well.

People argue, "Well, it's my body, so I can do what I want." It's pretty much the same way people who advocate abortion argue. Yet Saint Paul states, "Do you not know that your body is a temple of the Holy Spirit within you, which you have from God? You are not your own; you were bought with a price. So glorify God in your body" (1 Corinthians 6:19–20).

You and I are temples of the Holy Spirit, vessels to be kept sacred. We are all human and weak and fall into sin, but we are still temples of the Holy Spirit. But you argue,

"Even though it is a temple, it is still my body. And cannot I, therefore, do with it as I please?"

In the Gospel of Mark, Christ states, "Truly, I say to you, all sins will be forgiven the sons of men, and whatever blasphemies they utter, but whoever blasphemes against the Holy Spirit never has forgiveness, but is guilty of an eternal sin" (Mark 3:28–29). This is reiterated in the Gospel of Luke: "And every one who speaks a word against the Son of man will be forgiven; but he who blasphemes against the Holy Spirit will not be forgiven" (Luke 12:10).

What greater blasphemy could be possible than to destroy the temple of the Holy Spirit? No matter how difficult life becomes, the temple of the Holy Spirit must be preserved to the end. As Christ says, "But he who endures to the end will be saved" (Matt. 24:13).

What of the Old Testament? In the book of Exodus, God told Moses as he presented the world with his Ten Commandments, "You shall not kill" (Exod. 20:13). One supports the other! The Father supports the Son, and the Son supports the Father.

There may be exceptions, such as war, where one's total free will is influenced by extenuating circumstances (for example, going to war to stop the Hitlers of the world is necessary to preserve the sanctity of life).

God forbid that one should take a life to preserve a life. It is rather for me to keep sacred that temple of the Holy Spirit that dwells within. This I can do by the powers of my free will, but to consciously go out and destroy another being in whom a temple of the Holy Spirit dwells brings total and everlasting condemnation.

Remember, Christ said, "To blaspheme the Holy Spirit is a sin which will never be forgiven." To invade the temple of the Holy Spirit and to stop a life that is slowly and quietly growing under the protection of the Holy Spirit would seem to be the greatest of all blasphemies. It is of one's own free will to decide that a free will of another being shall not be considered. They call it "terminating the pregnancy" in order to avoid calling it by its true name: *murder!* They call it "freedom of choice" to avoid completing the sentence "Of my own free will, I choose to end that life that is growing within and for which a temple of the Holy Spirit shall be created in all its glory. A new dwelling place shall not, of my free choosing, be created. I do freely choose to blaspheme the Holy Spirit in this destruction of life, thus bringing upon myself a sin that will be carried to the end of my life." All of this then is left unsaid in the act of abortion, but it is heard by he who is omniscient.

Do we rely on only part of Scripture, accepting some and rejecting others, accepting that which is convenient to accept and rejecting that which is not? "First of all you must understand this, that no prophecy of Scripture is a matter of one's own interpretation, because no prophecy ever came by the impulse of man, but men moved by the Holy Spirit spoke from God." (2 Pet. 1:20–21). Although all of Scripture is influenced by the Holy Spirit, it is true that there are some passages that are difficult to fully comprehend. There is, however, no difficulty in understanding the statement "Whoever blasphemes against the Holy Spirit never has forgiveness." (Mark 3:29).

In summary, then, our bodies are temples of the Holy Spirit, and blasphemy of the Holy Spirit is a sin that is never to be forgiven. To kill the body is to destroy the temple of the Holy Spirit, and to do so of our own free will is to consciously blaspheme the Holy Spirit. To invade the temple of the Holy Spirit in order to kill a living being within, in which another temple of the Holy Spirit is being formed, is to create the greatest of all blasphemies.

Life is sacred, and to be pleasing to God, it should be thusly treated.

—February 27, 1995

10

THE LAST MIRACLE

THERE HE WAS, his face bleeding and his knees bruised from the falls, with an ignominious crown on his head, a crown of thorns that caused the blood to flow. A cross of wood was being carried by a man from Cyrene, signifying the death this man called Jesus was to die.

For the past three years, he had gone about the region doing good and teaching a new way of faith; he had even performed some miracles. Some had been cured of leprosy and some of blindness and deafness, and it is even reported that he raised a friend from death to life. One does not die for these acts; rather, he should be praised and admired. So it was, as there were those who would have made him their king. He resisted their efforts, yet he spoke of a kingdom of which he would rule. This, then, was one of his crimes; for in the time of Caesar, there was but one ruler, and that was Caesar. However, what really inflamed the people— the same people he had come to save—was that he made himself to be the Son of God. For this, the people would crucify him.

The procurator, Pilate, would have released him, but the people cried, "Let him be crucified." (Matt. 27:22). And thus, this man who preached forgiveness and love and who had performed extraordinary events (such as the feeding of so many from such little provisions) was led away to die a shameful death.

Was he to work no more miracles? Could he not work at least one more to save himself? It was not, however, to save himself that was his concern. Rather, he was to save millions by his death, and only by suffering on the cross was salvation to be had. Yet there was one more miracle to be given, one more miracle while he was still alive, an extraordinary event that was his silent way of saying, "I am Christ, Son of the living God. Follow me!"

The people did not see the presence of God in the feeding of five thousand. They did not see the Messiah in the raising of Lazarus from the dead. They did not see Christ in the curing of the lepers. Could they not see who he really was in the last miracle that was about to take place as he struggled up the road on his way to Golgotha?

He struggled, he stumbled along, and he fell. The blood by now was streaming down his face. The guards pushed and pulled to move him forward once again. There was a moment's hesitation; from out of the crowd, a young woman approached him with a cloth and tenderly and compassionately wiped the blood from his face. There on this veil of Veronica was left the image of the face of Jesus. There is no scriptural reference for this, only legend. Yet the cloth to this day is preserved in Rome.* But what if this extraordinary event of Jesus had been proclaimed on the housetops, would the people of that day have ceased from their desire to crucify him? It would have been highly unlikely, for his death was required for the salvation of our souls.

He was rejected then, and he is rejected now. For despite his miracles and teachings, even despite his rising from the

---

* The Collegiate Encyclopedia (New York: Grolier Inc., 1970) vol. 19, p. 72.

---- Reflections ----

dead, there are many who today re-crucify him by their actions. Is not sin a rejection of Christ? Is not sin a crucifixion of the one who called himself the living Son of God?

Today, one can either accept or reject him. That is the beauty of our free will. His last miracle was primarily a hidden one from the general population. But it remains for us today to see and understand that truly this was Christ. This nonverbal action of Christ speaks louder than any words that could have been uttered at that moment.

Christ cries out by his action, " Truly, truly, I say to you, before Abraham was, I am" (John 8:58).

—March 22, 1995

11

ON THE DIFFERENT LEVELS OF EXPERIENCING GOD

THE SEARCH FOR God, the complete and whole God in all his glory, is a long one. But in beginning a search for the Supreme Being, it means that one has been called to do so. It is not a verbal call by any means; rather, it is a call of the spirit.

One might begin his search in what has already been written—for example, the Holy Bible. In the Old Testament, we find a God who is severe—one who can allow the death of men, women, and children to accomplish his goal. He is a god who teaches—as God taught the Israelites—faith, obedience, trust, and the necessity to perform certain duties for his pleasure, such as the cleaning of bowls and the washing of hands in the preparation of a sacrifice. These outward signs are just some of the manifestations to God of one's love and fear of him.

All these, however, changed with the birth of Christ. A deeper level of the knowledge of God was now given to man. Now God is a deeply loving and compassionate god, a god who forgives man's weaknesses and has offered his only begotten Son for the forgiveness of the sins of mankind.

His Word became flesh to teach mankind the love of God and that it would be necessary for one's salvation. With the passing of Christ came faith, a faith that believes in the resurrection and eventual return of Christ.

Many went out into the desert to contemplate God and to experience him on an even deeper level. All are called to find him; but not all are called, or so it seems, to experience him on a deeper level. The transformation that is necessary in one's life to experience the omnipotent God is not one that all are willing to undergo. Scripture tells us, "My grace is sufficient for you, for my power of Christ may rest upon me" (2 Corinthians 12:9). One must be stripped of all outside influences in one's life in order to obtain an empty and weak state of being.

To see the face of God fills the person with his presence, but it is only with the knowledge of him that the person can comprehend. The omnipresent, omniscient, and omnipotent God is such that to know him in all his glory is more than any mere mortal can bear.

To see the face of God as the Song of Solomon states in 2:14, "Let me see your face", is to bring certain and immediate death. The strength of man's mortal heart cannot endure a total knowledge of the one true God and live. Yet God calls us to that knowledge. We put barriers in our way. We have our pastimes, hobbies, lives, entertainment, relationships, sex, work, etc. All these things, when taken appropriately, are good and necessary, yet they can stand in the way of the knowledge of God.

If one does not perform charitable works, then the search for God is more difficult, for Christ said, "Truly, I say to you, as you did it to one of the least of my brethren, you did it to me" (Matt. 25:40). So we must be charitable to those in need for this is a very important level of the knowledge and experience of God in our lives.

Contemplatives, such as Carthusian monks, perhaps experience God on a very profound level. They do nothing but contemplate his being each and every day. Then again, those who are out working with those in need also experience God on a very profound level. For each group, that level of experience can be enhanced to an even deeper level.

What of worldly needs? Can one spend one's total time in the experiencing of God with total disregard to material concerns? With faith in him—total faith—yes! Christ said, "But seek first his Kingdom and his righteousness, and all these things shall be yours as well" (Matt. 6:33). We hesitate, however, to this call; we seem to have it reversed.

We seek first the good life, and then we save one or two hours a week for him. This is what the world expects of us: to supply for the material life first. Then if time permits, we take care of the spiritual. To experience the presence of God on this level is only a very peripheral one.

The world, in its need to be both modern and rational, has lost sight of the need to be spiritual. A level of spirituality that exists only in the peripheral is almost nonexistent. But let us look where rationalism, in lieu of spirituality, has taken us.

There are those who are well off, who are at peace, and who enjoy life. But at the same time, there are those who are fighting to survive. Children who go hungry day after day, who have a street corner for a bed at night, and who must beg to survive are mingled with the blood of countries at war where atrocities abound. More compassion is given to a stranded whale than to a being made in the image of God. Mankind has confused its priorities.

In its need for independence and self-determination, mankind has given the approval of the worldwide slaughter of the unborn. Can any flower or any amoeba, moving and growing from its moment of creation, not have life? It staggers the imagination to believe that life begins only at birth. Was not that which is now totally formed into a human being in possession of life before its birth? While in the security of its mother's womb, did not this tiny creature have life from the moment of conception? Was not this life the beginning of a human being? Mankind feels comfortable with the death of this being by calling it the "termination of a fetus."

The woman's choice to terminate her pregnancy and to end her baby's growth brings to an end a soul of God on earth. But this soul still exists in the bosom of God, where it will be until the day of its mother's judgment, and then it will ask why.

To experience God on a deeper level than the one first encountered is to become aware of all that is written above. Mankind must seek out knowledge of the presence of God by answering the call it has received. Then this knowledge should be brought to an even deeper level, for this is what God is calling us to do.

—February 11, 1996

12

THE DESCENT OF THE HOLY SPIRIT

"And suddenly a sound came from heaven like the rush of a mighty wind, and it filled all the house where they were sitting. And there appeared to them tongues as of fire, distributed and resting on each one of them. And they were all filled with the Holy Spirit and began to speak in other tongues, as the Spirit gave them utterance" (Acts 2:2–4).

THUS THE TWELVE apostles—Matthias having replaced Judas, the betrayer—were so affected. Christ had been taken up into heaven prior to this experience of the Holy Spirit. It was now left to the apostles to proclaim the risen Christ. The success or failure of the church that Jesus had come into the world to establish rested on the shoulders of these twelve men.

Christ had told them while he was still in their presence that they would be receiving the Holy Spirit, but faith alone might not have been enough. In the coming days and weeks, the apostles would be experiencing many trials and persecutions, imprisonment, and even crucifixion. Something greater than faith, therefore, was needed. They had experienced the resurrection with their eyes and with their ears, but skeptics might have tried to convince the apostles that what they witnessed in the resurrection had been a ghost or a hallucination. More was needed, and more was received with the coming of Pentecost.

With the descent of the Holy Spirit, the sense of both sight and sound was realized. In addition to this came the actual physical experience of the indwelling of the Holy Spirit as the apostles began to make "bold proclamations" when they expressed themselves in tongues.

They had witnessed Christ in real life. They saw the miracles he performed. They understood his teachings, and now they experienced the power of his Holy Spirit since they had been left alone to carry out their mission. But they were not really alone, for Christ had told them, "I am with you always, to the close of the age." (Matt. 28:20).

—March 22, 1996

13

MY PERSONAL SEARCH FOR THE FACE OF GOD

IN THE EARLY 1970s, while I was attending Florida State University, I discovered a copy of a photograph that had been taken by a Japanese photographer. He had taken a picture of melting snow on the side of a mountain, perhaps Mount Fuji. At the time he took the picture, he did not observe anything unusual about the winter scene. When he developed the picture, however, he immediately noticed the face of Christ.

I spent many hours alone in my apartment, continuously looking at the photograph. Yet I was unable to find the face of Christ. Finally, in need of sustenance, I decided to put down the picture and go to dinner. As I was about to leave my apartment, I thought about giving the photograph to the lady next door to see if she could find what I had been unable to. My initial thoughts were "No, I want to find the face of Christ first, and then I will give the picture to her." As I left my apartment, having closed the door behind me, I came to the realization that the truly Christian and humble thing to do would be to give the picture to my neighbor. Therefore, I returned to my apartment, unlocked the door, entered, and, glancing at the table where I had left the picture; I immediately saw the face of Christ!

It is in this denying of self, this loving my neighbor, and becoming humble enough to place myself second to others that Christ revealed himself to me.

There is another story that I would like to share. Many years ago, perhaps in the late fifties or early sixties, I saw a movie entitled *The Silver Chalice*, starring Paul Newman. He portrayed a young and very talented artist, a sculptor. He had been commissioned by those who were in possession of the sacred cup that Christ had used at the Last Supper to sculpt around the cup the faces of Christ and the twelve apostles.

Some of the apostles he had known personally. Drawing and subsequently sculpting their faces around the circumference of the cup proved to be of no great difficulty. Others were described to him by those who had known them greatly, and again, sculpting their faces was not a difficult task.

When it came time to draw the face of Christ, the artist was unable to perform the task at hand. The artist had never known Jesus while he was alive, and although those who had known Jesus described him, he was unable to sculpt the face of Christ.

The completion of the cup was in need of only one more face, and until the artist had gone through a personal transformation in his own life, he would be unable to see the face of Christ. He told those who were waiting for the completed cup that this last face, the face of Christ, he had to see in his own mind. It was not like the others where people described the apostles to him, and he could easily draw them. Christ was different! He, as the Son of God, was a truth that the artist could not accept.

Finally, at the end of the movie, the actor had suffered much and was now able to accept Christ into his heart as his own personal Savior. He came to believe that Jesus was the Son of God. Now he was able to see and subsequently sculpt the face of Christ on the cup.

Reflections

The search for the face of God precedes the coming of Christ by many centuries. In the book of Exodus, Moses said, "I beg you, show me your glory" (Exod. 33:18). But God's response was, "...you cannot see my face; for man shall not see me and live" (Exod. 33:20). God went on to say that he would allow Moses to be in close proximity to him but that as his glory passed by, he would cover Moses's eyes with his hand for "...my face shall not be seen" (Exod. 33:23).

In the book of Kings, Elijah the prophet had been told to "Go forth, and stand upon the mount before the Lord" (1 Kings 19:11) for the Lord would be passing by. First came a strong and heavy wind, and the Lord was not there. Then came an earthquake, but again, the Lord was not there. Following this was a fire, and again, the Lord was not in the fire. Finally, there came "after the fire a still small voice. And when Elijah heard it, he wrapped his face in his mantle and went out and stood at the entrance of the cave" (Exod. 19:12–13).

Elijah was a prophet and a man of God, and he knew accordingly that if he were to look upon the face of God, he would surely die.

In the book of Psalms, there are many references to the face of God. To those who are faithful and just, God promises the reward of seeing his face: "...the upright shall behold his face" (Psalms 11:7).

Frequently, the psalmist cries out to the Lord. "How long, O Lord? Will you forget me forever? How long will you hide your face from me?" (Psalms 1) He knows that there is great consolation and comfort in the face of God. "Hear my prayer, O Lord; let my cry come to you! Do not hide your face from me in the day of my distress!" Psalms 102:1-2

Even though the psalmist knows that to look upon the face of God is to bring certain death, he still longs to gaze upon his Holy countenance. Yet God in his infinite wisdom does not permit such a thing to happen to those still in possession of their earthly life. Only in the next life, in the eternal life promised to his faithful, will God allow us to see his divine face.

When Christ was alive, Philip asked Jesus to show him the Father; and Jesus replied, "He who has seen me has seen the Father" (John 14:9).

There is a slight problem here, for if we look at the face of Jesus, we will not die; yet if we look at the face of God his Father, we will die. How then can we look at the face of Jesus and not see the Father?

As in the birth of any child, there is always some resemblance of the father responsible for his or her birth. God the Holy Spirit overshadowed the Virgin Mary, and she gave birth. Christ then has the resemblance of God the Father for he is truly his Son! Yet to behold the glory of God is not for mortal man, but only for eternal life.

It is God who calls us in this life: "Seek my face." The psalmist responds, "Your face, Lord, do I seek" (Ps. 27:8). In the very next verse, the psalmist pleads with God: "Hide not your face from me" (Psalm 9).

Thus it should be with each and every one of us: to seek the face of God. There are different levels of spirituality, as explained in an earlier essay. There are also different levels of experiencing Christ among the many faces of Christ that we encounter. There is the face of Christ in the simple beggar. There is the face of Christ that Mother Teresa of Calcutta saw each day in the abandoned and starving child. There is the face of Christ in the humble and repentant sinner who has come to accept Christ as his personal Savior, and there is the face of Christ in the broken body and spirit of the long-forgotten resident of a nursing home.

As we deal with each of these encounters in our own life, we experience Christ's presence. If we then allow Christ to come into our life through the needs of our neighbor, we begin to experience God on a deeper level. He then calls us to seek his divine face. We must not hesitate in our search even though we know that to accomplish our goal would bring certain death. All our trust must be placed in God, who will overshadow us with his love as he brings us to eternal life.

Perhaps this trust is what Christ meant when he said that we must become as little children in order to enter into the kingdom of God; that is, search for the face of God as a child looks for his mother upon rising in the morning. Search for God as you give what you really can't afford to give to someone in greater need than you.

Search for the face of God as did Saint Francis of Assisi as he kissed the leper who was repugnant to him. Search for the face of God as you forgive those who have wronged you, as did the Son of God crucified on a wooden cross.

Search for the face of God each and every moment of every day. Let nothing deter you or stand in your way, and your journey toward your heart's desire will one day be fulfilled.

—October 6, 1996

14

MEDITATIONS ON THE HOLY ROSARY

MANY PEOPLE HAVE difficulty concentrating on the mysteries of the Rosary. In order to prevent this from happening, a suggestion is made. If one were to consider one aspect of each mystery and then let the Lord lead you wherever he may, there would be fewer distractions; and our Lady, the Virgin Mother, would be greatly pleased.

Case in point: while saying the Joyful Mysteries (in particular, the fourth mystery: The Presentation), the following thought came to me. When Saint Joseph and Mary took Jesus to the temple to present him to the Lord, did they really appreciate whom they were presenting? Mary was told by the angel Gabriel that Jesus would be the "Son of the Most High," and Saint Joseph was told also by an angel that "...he will save his people from their sins" (Matt. 1:21). But I wonder if they really appreciated the fact that that baby was not only Son of God but God as well, for as Jesus said, "I and the Father are one" (John 10:30).

Now let's take the Sorrowful Mysteries. In particular, let us look at the fourth mystery: The Way of the Cross. One might meditate on the individual stations of the cross as one repeats the Hail Mary, or one might consider the weight of the cross and the great wound that must have resulted on his shoulder. The pain must have been excruciating. Perhaps not at first, but with each step he took, the wood would have cut into his shoulder. There would have been no compassion for him as the soldiers pushed him along the way to Golgotha, and surely they would have seen not only the blood flowing from the spot where the heavy cross rested but also the grimace on his face the further they went. Finally, let us look at the Glorious Mysteries. Again, let us look at the fourth mystery: The Assumption. Jesus had given Mary to the disciple he loved, John: "Woman, behold your son!" Then he said to the disciple, "Behold, your mother!" (John 19:26-27) Therefore, Mary lived with John until her death. But here was the mother of God; her body could not corrupt in the grave, and she had work to do (that is, her many appearances on earth throughout the centuries). She was therefore assumed into heaven to await her glorious coronation, which is the final mystery.

—November 11, 1998